FIESTA!

NICARAGUA

GROLIER

An Imprint of Scholastic Library Publishing
Danbury, Connecticut

Published for Grolier
an imprint of Scholastic Library Publishing
Old Sherman Turnpike, Danbury, Connecticut 06816
by Marshall Cavendish Editions
an imprint of Marshall Cavendish International
1 New Industrial Road, Singapore 536196

Set ISBN: 0-7172-5788-6
Volume ISBN: 0-7172-5797-5

Library of Congress Cataloging-in-Publication Data
Nicaragua.
p. cm.—(Fiesta!)
Summary: Discusses the festivals and holidays of Nicaragua and how the songs, food,
and traditions associated with these celebrations reflect the culture of the people.
1. Festivals—Nicaragua—Juvenile literature. 2. Nicaragua—Social life and customs—Juvenile literature.
[1. Festivals—Nicaragua. 2. Holidays—Nicaragua. 3. Nicaragua—Social life and customs.]
I. Grolier (Firm). II. Fiesta! (Danbury, Conn.)
GT4820.A2N53 2004
394.267285—dc21   2003044847

For this volume
Author: Yumi Ng
Editor: Krisinder Kaur
Designer: Ang Lee Ming
Production: Nor Sidah Haron
Crafts and Recipes produced by Stephen Russell

Printed by Everbest Printing Co. Ltd

Adult supervision advised for all crafts and recipes,
particularly those involving sharp instruments and heat.

CONTENTS

NICARAGUA:

Nicaragua is the largest country in Central America. Some people say the name Nicaragua means "here by the water" in an ancient Amerindian language.

HONDURAS

EL SALVADOR

Lake Managua

Masaya Volcano

Cerro Negro

León

MANAGUA

Masaya

Granada

PACIFIC OCEAN

Diriamba

▲ **Lake Managua and Lake Nicaragua** are two large lakes located near the western coast of Nicaragua. Managua, Nicaragua's capital city, is located along the southern shore of Lake Managua.

▶ **Volcanoes** cause earthquakes and eruptions in Nicaragua, sometimes destroying homes and villages. There are more than 10 active volcanoes and many more inactive volcanoes in Nicaragua.

Mosquito Coast

NICARAGUA

CARIBBEAN
SEA

Lake Nicaragua

San Juan River

COSTA RICA

▲ **Catholic churches** in Nicaragua house beautiful images of Jesus, the Virgin Mary, and the saints. The cathedral in the city of León is the largest church in Central America.

▶ **Corn** is the main ingredient in many delicious Nicaraguan dishes such as tortillas and nacatamales, a tasty corn meal dish filled with rice, cheese, ground meat, and hot peppers, and wrapped tightly in banana leaves.

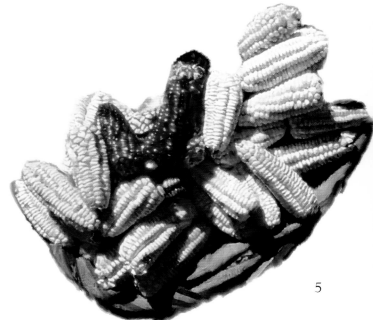

RELIGIONS

The majority of Nicaraguans are Roman Catholics. There is also a small group of Protestants in the country.

MOST NICARAGUANS are Roman Catholics. In the early 1500s Spanish soldiers called conquistadors arrived in Nicaragua and conquered the land. The people living in Nicaragua at that time were the Nicarao, an Amerindian people related to the Aztec and Maya peoples of Mexico. The Nicarao worshiped nature and believed in many gods that controlled nature, such as the sun and rain gods. The Nicarao also worshiped corn, since it was their main source of food.

The Spanish were Roman Catholics and built many beautiful churches in the Spanish style in Nicaragua. The biggest Catholic cathedral in Central America is located in León, a city in Nicaragua. Nicaraguans also celebrate special Catholic holidays such as the Immaculate Conception of Mary.

Although the Spanish succeeded in converting most of the Nicarao to Christianity, the Amerindians kept some of their beliefs and mixed them with Christian traditions. For example, some people say that the Nicarao accepted Christianity because the symbol of their god of rain, Tlaloc, had four arms, making it look similar to a cross. As the years went by, the Nicarao combined some of the rituals of their own religion into their practice of the Catholic faith.

Every city and town in the country honors a patron saint who they believe will grant them special requests and protect them from harm. Nicaraguans hold special festivals to honor these patron saints every year.

Although the Spanish soldiers gained complete possession of the western coast of Nicaragua and its people, they did not venture as far as the Mosquito

Coast located on the eastern side of Nicaragua. Groups of Miskito, Rama, and Sumo Amerindians living there were able to continue speaking their own language and practice their native religion. The British took control of the Mosquito Coast in the 1600s and introduced Protestantism to the people living there. Today quite a number of Nicaraguans living on the Atlantic Coast are members of the Protestant church.

GREETINGS FROM **NICARAGUA!**

Nicaraguans call themselves "Nicas," and they speak Spanish. Before the Spanish came to Nicaragua, the Nicarao Amerindians spoke a language that was similar to the languages of the Maya and Aztec peoples in Mexico and Guatemala. Today the language of the Nicarao has almost disappeared, and Spanish is spoken by the majority of the people in Nicaragua.

How do you say...

Hello
Hola

How are you?
Cómo estás?

My name is
Me llamo

Homeland
Patria

Thank you
Gracias

SAINT SEBASTIAN FESTIVAL

Many Nicaraguan cities have a patron saint. Nicaraguans believe that patron saints protect their cities from natural disasters such as earthquakes and erupting volcanoes, and also help people in times of need.

Saint Sebastian is the patron saint of Diriamba, and the people living there celebrate his festival on January 20. Nobody really knows how this saint came to be Diriamba's patron saint, but the residents of Diriamba have been celebrating his festival for hundreds of years.

Saint Sebastian lived in the third century A.D. in Rome, the capital of the powerful Roman Empire. The Christians in Rome at that time were often badly treated and sent to prison by the Roman Emperor Diocletian. Sebastian was a young Christian man who decided to join the Roman army so that he could go into the prisons and secretly help the Christians. Sebastian brought food, water, and comfort to the Christian prisoners for a while, but

Diocletian found out and had Sebastian punished. Diocletian ordered that Sebastian be tied to a tree and shot with arrows. But Sebastian was able to survive the punishment. Sebastian then attempted to meet Diocletian to talk to him about the Christian faith. The proud emperor, however, refused to listen and ordered that Sebastian be beaten to death.

The people living in Diriamba celebrate the festival of Saint Sebastian by attending a special mass. After the mass the people bring out the image of Saint Sebastian and carry it on their shoulders in a procession. The image is a statue that shows the saint's body pierced with sharp arrows.

Nicaraguans celebrate this festival with special dances. The *toro huaco* is the most popular dance. The main dancer in the group wears a cow mask and a hat with horns.

Toro in Spanish means bull. Musicians play the flute and the drums, two ancient Amerindian instruments, to accompany the dance. Other dances are also performed in the festive procession. El Güegüense dancers wear masks of old Spanish soldiers and tall hats decorated with colorful paper flowers.

The dancers also wear long capes, such as those the conquistadors wore. Nicaraguans believe this dance started as a way for the Amerindians to make fun of their Spanish rulers. Many of the participants in the festival are people whose prayers have been answered. In gratitude, they promise to honor the saint by performing dances during his festival.

Groups of festival musicians called *chicheros* play traditional tunes on the marimba, a popular musical instrument in Nicaragua. The *chicheros* bring cheer and joy to the festival.

The people of Diriamba go to church and light a candle to show their love and respect for Saint Sebastian. At the festival procession they blow on paper horns, shake noisy rattles, and play instruments such as the drum to add cheer to the festival.

MAKE A COLORFUL EL GÜEGÜENSE HAT

YOU WILL NEED

A large wide-brimmed straw hat
Brightly colored sheets of paper
Masking tape
Measuring tape
Old newspaper
Oil pastels or other paints in bright colors
Different size brushes
6 feet of yellow cloth ribbon with tassels
6 feet of yellow satin ribbon
Long needle and light-color thread
Peacock feathers

During the festival of Saint Sebastian Nicaraguan men perform a dance called El Güegüense. The dancers wear tall, colorful hats and masks that look like the faces of the Spanish men who conquered Nicaragua centuries ago. Why not make your own tall hat and wear it during a festival in your city or town?

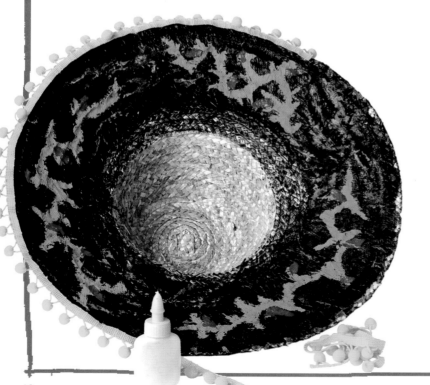

1 Paint colorful designs on the inside brim of the hat. After you are finished, let the paint dry by placing the hat face up.

2 To thread the ribbon, make two 1" slits on opposite sides of the hat's top right at the border between the top and the brim. Thread one end of the yellow ribbon through one slit and the other end through the other slit. Make sure the two ends of the ribbon hang down evenly from the inside of the hat.

4 Measure the edge of the hat using the measuring tape. Then cut the ribbon with the tassels to the same length. Attach the ribbon to the brim using a needle and some thread. Stick the peacock feathers to the top of the hat using the masking tape. Now you can put on your new hat.

3 Crumple up newspaper sheets into several balls. Then cover each ball with a different piece of colored paper. Make sure to secure each ball with a small piece of tape. Stick the balls all around the top of the hat using masking tape.

SEMANA SANTA

Semana Santa is also known as Holy Week. Nicaraguans have various celebrations during this week to celebrate Easter. Part of the celebrations involve acting out a scene from the Bible and remembering the sufferings of Jesus Christ.

In March or April each year people in Nicaragua celebrate Easter, the Christian holiday that honors the death and resurrection of Jesus Christ. The Semana Santa, or Holy Week, festival lasts the entire week and ends with Easter Sunday celebrations.

This bronze image is taken from a painting called "The Last Supper" that shows Jesus Christ having his final meal with the 12 apostles.

When Jesus Christ entered the city of Jerusalem riding a donkey, many people lined the streets to welcome him.

The celebrations begin on Palm Sunday. Priests bless palm leaves during Mass and give the leaves to the people, who hold the palm leaves in their hands and follow a procession around town. An image of Jesus Christ sitting on a donkey is carried during the procession. The image

Cheese soup is one of the special dishes Nicaraguans eat during Semana Santa.

of Jesus Christ from the dead. This is the most important event for all Christians. Nicaraguans celebrate by eating special food such as cheese soup and sardines. As a form of personal sacrifice, they do not eat red meat during Semana Santa.

reminds people of the day Jesus Christ entered the city of Jerusalem in Israel riding on a donkey's back. Nicaraguans keep the palm leaves for a few days, since they believe the palms will protect their homes.

The next three days are mostly days for prayer and attending a special mass to pray for the sick. On Thursday the people commemorate the Last Supper, when Jesus Christ washed the feet of the apostles and shared bread and wine with them for the last time before his death. Many churchgoers make a silent procession around the town.

Good Friday is one of the most important days of Holy Week. Nicaraguans remember the day Jesus was crucified to pay for the sins of the world and bring salvation to people. Priests celebrate special masses to thank God for the sacrifice of Jesus Christ. In some towns in Nicaragua people act out plays about the last days of Jesus Christ.

On Saturday churches across Nicaragua organize processions. In the evening groups of people gather in church for a solemn vigil.

Easter Sunday is a time of joy and celebration for Nicaraguans as they remember the resurrection

In Christianity wine is used to represent the blood of Jesus Christ.

13

FESTIVAL OF SAINT LAZARUS

Saint Lazarus was a man who endured great suffering. He was treated badly by a rich man. During the festival of Saint Lazarus the people of Monimbó attend Mass and have parades in memory of his hardships.

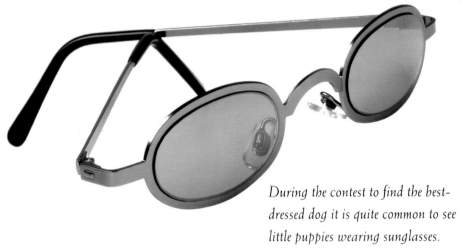

During the contest to find the best-dressed dog it is quite common to see little puppies wearing sunglasses.

The people of the village of Monimbó in the Masaya district celebrate the festival of Saint Lazarus in March, a week before Palm Sunday. Before celebrations begin, a statue of Saint Lazarus is brought down from a special niche in Saint Mary Magdalene Church, where it is kept throughout the year.

People in Monimbó believe that Saint Lazarus will help those with skin diseases and protect dogs and puppies. The image of Saint Lazarus shows the saint with scars on his arms and legs, walking with a cane. A dog is standing by his side. This image of him comes from a story in the Bible. Lazarus was a poor man with many sores on his body. He used to sit outside the home of a rich man asking for help and food to eat. But the rich man did not pay attention to him and even let his dogs lick Lazarus's wounds and sores.

During the feast of Saint Lazarus Nicaraguans light candles made from animal fat and place them at the foot of the image of the saint. They pray to the saint and wait until the candle melts. Those who suffer from skin diseases rub the melted wax on their skin, believing that the wax can heal them. Those who have been healed by the saint in previous years come to

Dog owners parade their dressed-up pets in the hope of winning prizes during the festival of Saint Lazarus.

church walking on their knees while others buy silver charms to show the saint how thankful they are for his healing.

In Monimbó people also bring food to the priests and other church workers on this day to thank them for their work in the church throughout the year.

The most interesting event during this festival is the parade and contest for the best-dressed dog. People clothe their dogs in dresses, T-shirts, hats, sunglasses, and other costumes. Judges then choose the best-dressed dog and give out prizes to the winners.

Everyone present at the contest enjoys the food, music, and dancing, as a band of *chiceros* plays tunes on their marimbas.

15

MAKE A MINI MARIMBA

YOU WILL NEED

Old newspaper
5 thick straws with "accordion bends"
4 thin straws with "accordion bends"
Brown construction paper
1 sheet of aluminum foil
Black masking tape and scotch tape
Paper fasteners and thin wire
Thick string
Thin cardboard
Needle and thread

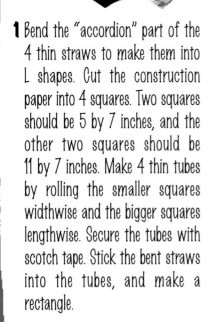

Marimba players bring joyful music to all Nicaraguan festivals! You can make your own marimba by using straws.

2 Cut the wires into 7-inch pieces. Wind each piece of wire around the bends. These wires will later be attached to the legs of your mini marimba.

3 Cut each thick straw in half. With the needle pierce two small holes opposite each other near the top of each straw. Using the needle and thread, link the straws together by inserting the thread through the holes in the straws.

1 Bend the "accordion" part of the 4 thin straws to make them into L shapes. Cut the construction paper into 4 squares. Two squares should be 5 by 7 inches, and the other two squares should be 11 by 7 inches. Make 4 thin tubes by rolling the smaller squares widthwise and the bigger squares lengthwise. Secure the tubes with scotch tape. Stick the bent straws into the tubes, and make a rectangle.

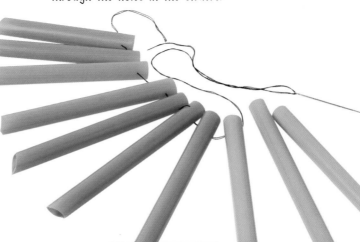

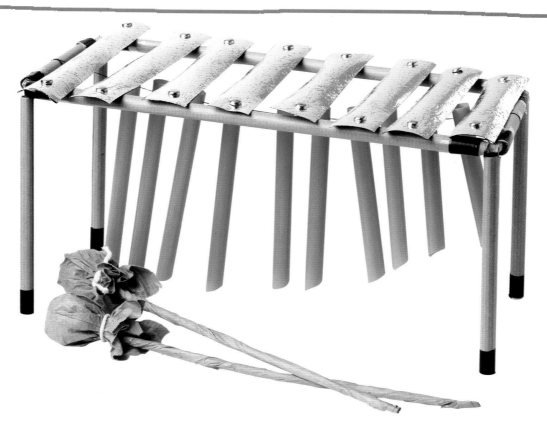

4 Make the keys of the marimba by cutting out rectangular pieces of black cardboard in 8 different sizes, ranging from 6 to 13 inch-long rectangles. Glue strips of aluminum foil onto the cardboard strips, and roll the strips slightly so that they curl. Poke the fasteners into place on both ends of the strips.

5 Make the drumsticks by covering two straws with construction paper. Roll two balls out of old newspaper, and fasten them to one end of the sticks with scotch tape. Cover the balls with a square piece of construction paper, and secure it onto the ball by tying a piece of string around it.

6 Make the legs of the marimba by rolling 4 pieces of brown paper each measuring 11 by 7 inches. Secure the legs with scotch tape. Now take the frame of the marimba, and insert the wires hanging down from each corner into the legs.

7 Tape the lower part of the legs and other parts shown in the picture with a piece of black tape. Glue the keys onto the top of the marimba. Finally, tie up the strings of the tube onto the short sides of the frame to complete your mini marimba.

INDEPENDENCE DAY

Nicaragua celebrates its independence over two days, September 14 and 15, every year. Many schools organize street parades with music, dance, and fireworks displays.

After the arrival of the first Spanish conquistadors in Nicaragua in the 1500s, Nicaraguans lived under Spanish rule for 300 years. The Amerindians of Nicaragua were treated harshly by the Spanish rulers. They forced the Nicaraguans to work hard without giving them any education or pay.

In the early 1800s most Spanish colonies in Latin America wanted to achieve independence from Spain. They felt that they could rule their own countries. The French and American revolutions also inspired many of these countries to fight for their own freedom. In the early 1820s Mexico and Peru, Spain's largest colonies in Latin America, became independent after fighting and defeating the Spanish armies. Nicaragua and other Central American colonies declared their independence from Spain in 1821. At first Nicaragua became a member of the Mexican empire, but it joined the United Provinces of Central

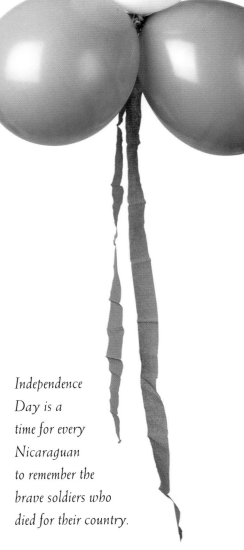

Independence Day is a time for every Nicaraguan to remember the brave soldiers who died for their country.

America one year later. Nicaragua declared independence in 1838.

In the 1850s an American, William Walker, took over the governing of the country and made himself president.

Many Nicaraguans did not want William Walker to be their president, so they formed an army to drive him out of the country. They defeated Walker and his army in the Battle of San Jacinto on September 14 and 15, 1856, which are now the national days of Nicaragua. On both September 14 and 15 every year many schools throughout Nicaragua organize grand parades in which school bands and dancers perform. When the national anthem is sung, everybody stops and stands at attention. The mayor of the city then gives speeches that honor and remember those Nicaraguans who died for their country's freedom. The celebrations end with a spectacular display of fireworks.

HIMNO NACIONAL

Hail to you, Nicaragua!
The cannon's voice no longer roars,
Nor does the blood of our brothers
Stain your glorious bicolored flag.

FESTIVAL OF SAINT JEROME

Saint Jerome is the patron saint of the city of Masaya, and the people celebrate the saint's festival from September to December each year. It is the longest festival in Nicaragua.

During special festivals Nicaraguans display traditional crafts for sale at outdoor markets.

Saint Jerome lived in Rome during the early years of the Christian church. It was he who translated the Bible from Hebrew to Latin.

The people of Masaya began celebrating the festival of Saint Jerome during the colonial period of Spanish rule. In those days the Amerindians made use of festivals to create dances in which they could make fun of their Spanish rulers. The Amerindians mixed their traditional music, dances, and costumes with Spanish traditions during the celebrations. In this way the Spanish colonists and soldiers did not realize that these dances were actually being performed in order to make fun of them.

One of these dances is the dance of the *torovenados*. *Torovenados* means "bull-deer." The bull represents the strength of the Spanish conquistadors, and the deer represents the quickness and shrewdness of the Amerindians. The name Masaya actually means "place of the deer" in the ancient language of the Amerindians.

Nicaraguans still make fun of the leaders of their government or other international politicians during special festivals.

During the festival of Saint Jerome the people of Masaya take part in the *torovenados* parade dressed in outrageous costumes. They wear old-fashioned

clothes, funny masks, and sometimes even carry broken umbrellas. They imitate the gestures and movements of the Spanish leaders. Dancers dressed in costumes representing a character that is half-bull and half-deer also take part in the parade. A group of people called the *Negras* dress in black outfits and white masks and perform another type of dance. Traditionally only men take part in this dance, so half the men dress up as women. A musical band plays traditional songs to accompany the dance. The people of Masaya set off firecrackers as the parade passes along the streets of the city.

A pair of bulls pulling a small float decorated with coconut palms and colorful paper banners form the main part of the parade procession. At the end of the procession is an image of Saint Jerome that is carried on the shoulders of those who have asked the saint for a special favor, such as the healing of a disease, and been granted their wish.

The deer is an important symbol to the city of Masaya.

MAZAPANES

SERVES 6

1 cup ground sugar
1 cup ground almonds
2 tbsp water
1 egg white
Raisins

2 Using an electric mixer, mix egg white until it turns into a soft foam. Dip cooking brush into foam, and coat each shape with egg white. Preheat oven to 360 degrees Farenheit.

3 Place baking tray in oven, and bake for about 2 minutes. Remove tray from oven, and serve on a plate. Decorate with raisins.

1 Put sugar, almonds, and water in a bowl. Using your hands, mix well until mixture becomes a dough. Make small hearts and any other shape you want with the dough. Place the shapes on a baking tray.

THE OLD WOMAN OF MASAYA VOLCANO

This is a tale of an old woman who could see into the future.
She lived in a crater at the bottom of a volcano
and was highly respected among the native people.

A LONG TIME AGO, before the Spanish conquistadors arrived in Nicaragua, groups of Amerindians lived together. These groups had their own leaders called caciques. An Amerindian group called the Chorotegas lived near the Masaya Volcano. The Chorotegas called this volcano Popogatepe, which means "burning mount" in their language.

The Chorotegas claimed that a wise old woman lived right at the bottom of one of the craters of the volcano. People who had seen this woman said she was wrinkled and ugly, with tangled hair. The caciques, however, respected the woman because they said she could see the future.

Before the caciques declared war on neighboring groups, they would send their men to ask the old woman who would win the war. The men would stop at the edge of Popogatepe's deepest crater, and the old woman would climb out to talk to them. If the old woman told them that they would lose the war, the caciques would wait for a luckier time to attack.

The old woman also advised the caciques about how much food they would be able to harvest every year, as well as when earthquakes and eruptions were going to take place. She also knew when good fortune and wealth would be granted to a person, and so the caciques grew to trust the old woman completely.

When news of the arrival of the Spanish reached the ears of the caciques, they did not know what to do. Anxiously they went to the crater to find out what the old woman had to say. She told them

that the white men were evil, and that she would not come out of the crater until the white men were driven out of the land.

After the Spanish conquered the land, they went up to the crater where the old woman lived and, on seeing the burning lava, thought it was the entrance to hell.

A Catholic priest called Francisco de Bobadilla had heard stories about the old woman. Fearing that she could be a witch or the devil in person, he immediately placed a wooden cross at the foot of the crater. After that the old woman was never seen or heard of again.

ALL SAINTS' AND ALL SOULS' DAYS

All Saints' Day is celebrated on November 1 and All Souls' Day on November 2. All Saints' Day honors Catholic saints, and All Souls' Day is a time to remember the souls of people who have died.

Nicaraguans celebrate All Saints' Day by going to church and praying to the patron saint of their town. Catholics believe that every saint helps people in a special way. To show their respect for the saints, Nicaraguans light candles and place them near the statues of the saints in the church.

The next day, November 2, is All Souls' Day. On this day Nicaraguans go to the cemetery to visit the graves of their family members and relatives. They wake up very early in the morning, prepare a picnic meal, and carry the meal as well as bouquets of flowers to the cemetery. The family arranges the fresh flowers around the grave and sits by the grave to have their picnic. Sometimes the family may bring special food and put it around the grave. This is not a Catholic practice, but Nicaraguans believe it will make the soul of the dead relative happy.

Nicaraguans put flowers on the graves of their loved ones on All Souls' Day.

GALLO PINTO

SERVES 6

1 cup red kidney beans
4¼ cups water
1 bay leaf
1 small red onion, peeled and washed
3 garlic cloves, peeled
Salt
3 tbsp vegetable oil
1 small red onion, chopped
1 small red pepper
3 cups rice, cooked
2 tbsp chopped cilantro
Sour cream and slices of avocado

1 Pick whole, firm beans. Wash beans thoroughly, and let them soak overnight in water in a covered pot. Drain beans, and put them in a cooking pot with 4 cups of water. Add the bay leaf, 1 peeled onion, and 2 garlic cloves to pot. Cover pot with a lid, and bring to a boil. Cook for 1 hour until beans are tender.

2 Add a pinch of salt during the last 10 minutes of cooking time. (If salt is added before, beans will harden.) Get an adult to help you remove pot from heat, and discard water, onion, bay leaf, and garlic. Wash beans briefly in cold water.

3 Heat oil in a pan, and add chopped onions and red pepper. Fry onions and red pepper in medium heat until soft. Smash 1 garlic clove, and add to mixture.

Fry for one more minute, and add cooked rice to onion mixture. Fry rice with onion mixture for about 1 minute.

4 Add beans and ¼ cup water to rice and onion mixture, and cook for about 10 minutes, mixing ingredients until rice turns red. Remove from heat, and combine chopped cilantro with rice and beans. Serve rice and beans with a dollop of sour cream and avocado slices.

LA PURÍSIMA

La Purísima is celebrated in every part of Nicaragua. It is an important festival celebrating the Immaculate Conception of Mary.

People are invited into homes to pray at the altar set up by the family. They also sing songs that praise the Virgin Mary.

La Purísima is one of the most important celebrations for Catholics in Nicaragua. This holiday honors the Immaculate Conception of the Virgin Mary.

Catholics believe that Mary was born without sin because she was to be the mother of Jesus Christ. *La Purísima* means "The Extremely Pure One" in Spanish, and it is one of the many affectionate ways Nicaraguans refer to the Virgin Mary. Nicaraguans generally celebrate La Purísima on December 6 and 7, but in some places like Managua the festivities start on December 1 and last for one week.

Some people say that the tradition of celebrating the festival of La Purísima started hundreds of years ago during the Spanish colonial period. According to legend, one day the Cerro Negro Volcano erupted, and it spilled lava for days. The people of León were worried because the volcano was very near their city, and they were afraid the lava would harm their homes. Not knowing what to do, the people decided to bring a statue of the Virgin Mary and place it on the ground at the foot of the volcano. Then a

Little children ask the Virgin Mary to keep them safe and to bless them.

Paper boxes (below) filled with sweets are given to children who visit homes during La Purísima. Some people give out fruits, vegetables, and sugarcane to other visitors.

miracle occurred. The volcano suddenly stopped spewing lava. The people were so overjoyed and grateful to the Virgin Mary for the miracle that they decided to make a special celebration on the day of Mary's Immaculate Conception.

Since that time the tradition of celebrating La Purísima has become one of the liveliest festivals in Nicaragua. People set up altars in their homes where they place a statue or an image of the Virgin. They decorate the altars with flowers, candles, and Christmas lights. On December 7 groups of adults and children go from house to house singing songs, playing

with firecrackers, and shouting before every door, "What brings us so much joy?" The hosts then reply, "The Conception of Mary!" The hosts give each child a paper box called a *paquete* filled with sweets. Little wonder, then, that December 7 is called *la gritería*, or "the shouting," among the people of Nicaragua.

Churches and shops also set up very beautiful and elaborate altars in their premises or on the street so that people passing by can pay their respects to the Virgin. In the city of Managua the

La Purísima celebrations end with a spectacular fireworks display. People from all over Nicaragua visit Managua to view the fireworks.

THE STORY OF THE VIRGIN OF THE CONCEPTION

A mysterious box is found floating in the waters of Lake Nicaragua, and inside it is a beautiful statue of the Virgin Mary. The statue is said to protect the people of Granada from harm until this very day.

IN THE CITY of Granada long ago in 1712 a group of women made a surprising discovery. They were washing their laundry in the waters of Lake Nicaragua when suddenly they spotted a large wooden box floating in the water. The women stopped their washing and stared at the strange box. Curious to see what was in it, they tried to grab it to bring it to shore. But the box kept floating away. The more they tried to grab it, the more it slipped from their hands. Fearing that the box might be possessed by the devil, the women went to seek help from the priests at the Convent of St. Francis.

The priests followed the women down to the lake to see if this mysterious box was indeed possessed by the devil as the women had claimed. The priests went into the water to fetch the box, and to everyone's surprise the strange box floated straight toward them.

The excited priests quickly pulled the heavy box to shore. As they lifted the heavy wooden lid, the crowd gasped in amazement. Inside they found a beautiful wooden image of the Virgin with the Baby Jesus in her arms.

Everyone rejoiced at such a blessed discovery, and word spread through the town. The bishop of Nicaragua named the image "The Conception of Mary." He agreed to put it in a church in Granada.

Nobody knows where the box came from, but the people of Granada believe that the image has protected the city of Granada. In one incident English pirates tried to invade Granada by sailing up

the San Juan River in their ships. The Conception Castle that was built as a fort against the invaders saved the city from being conquered by the English.

This victory and many others are attributed to the Virgin Mary, who is believed to protect Granada and its people with her blessings.

CHRISTMAS

Christmas is called Navidad in Spanish. Since most Nicaraguans are Christians, the birth of Jesus Christ is a special holiday in Nicaragua.

Nicaraguans usually celebrate Christmas, or *Navidad*, with their families and close friends. Before Christmas families paint their houses and put up Christmas decorations. On Christmas Eve they spend hours in the kitchen preparing the Christmas Eve meal, which may be roasted chicken or turkey with stuffing. They also prepare a special treat called *nacatamales*, made with corn flour, chicken or pork, onions, rice, and spices that are wrapped together in a banana leaf and steamed. Bread and special cakes are also baked for the family and their guests to enjoy.

After the Christmas Eve meal families attend mass together in church. At midnight they hug one another. This special hug is called the *abrazos de paz*, or "hug of peace." They then pray for peace in their homes and across the land. Nicaraguans also sing a few traditional Christmas songs which are known as *villancicos*. They set off firecrackers at night. Sometimes the festivities can continue all through the night until the next morning.

On Christmas day children wait for the God Child, who they believe will bring them presents if they are good. They also receive presents from their parents and godparents.

WORDS TO KNOW

Amerindians: The people who lived in North, Central, and South America before the arrival of the Europeans.

Apostles: The first followers of Jesus Christ.

Chicheros: Street musicians who play in a band during festivals.

Colony: A group of people who live in a territory far away from the land of their rulers.

Conquistadors: Spanish adventurers who came to the Americas in the 16th century and conquered most parts of Central and South America.

Convert: To get a people to believe in a religion other than the one they already believe in.

Hebrew: The language in which the Old Testament books of the Bible were written.

Immaculate: Pure, without stain.

Latin: The ancient language of the Roman empire; the language on which French, Italian, Portuguese, Romanian, and Spanish are based.

Lava: The molten rock that flows from a volcano.

Lunar calendar: A calendar that is based on the revolutions of the moon. It is divided into 12 lunar months. Each lunar month is often shorter than 30 days.

Niche: A recess in a wall, especially for a statue.

Procession: A line of people moving in an orderly manner during a ceremony or religious ritual.

Resurrection: The act of rising from death.

Revolution: A movement by the people to overthrow and replace the existing government.

Vigil: The act of keeping watch through the night, usually the night before a religious festival.

ACKNOWLEDGMENTS

WITH THANKS TO:
Ali Akbar Kasim, Bezaleel Arvind, Katharine Brown, Muhammad Akid Durrani Imran, Stella Rodrigues, Sunita Geet Kaur, Susan Jane Manuel, and R. Senthamarai

PHOTOGRAPHS BY:
Haga Library, Japan (cover), Sam Yeo (pp. 6-7, pp. 14-15, p. 19 top left, pp. 20-21, p. 24, p. 26), Ben Yap (p. 9, p. 12 lower right, p. 18 lower left, p. 19 lower right), and Yu Hui Ying (all others)

ILLUSTRATIONS BY:
Ang Lee Ming (p. 1, pp. 4-5, p. 7), Lee Kowling (p. 29), and Ong Lay Keng (p. 23)

Set Contents